ppens in

ent

Citizen Guides

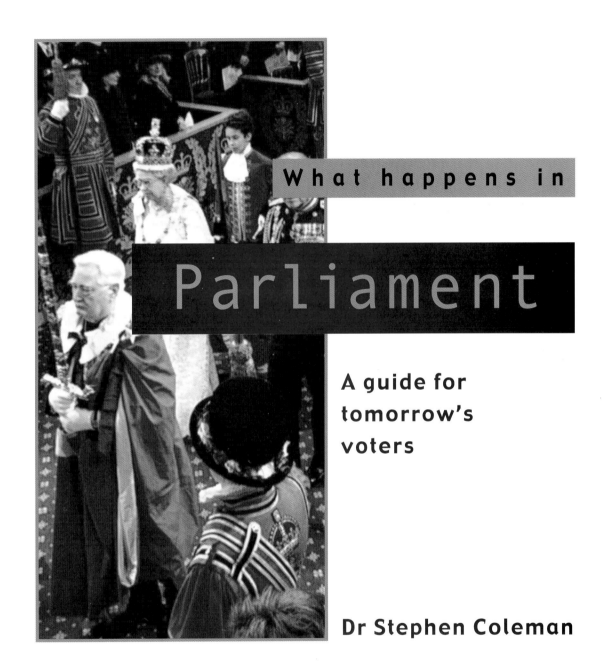

What happens in

Parliament

A guide for tomorrow's voters

Dr Stephen Coleman

FRANKLIN WATTS
LONDON • SYDNEY

About the author
Dr Stephen Coleman is Director of Studies at The Hansard Society and specialises in examining politics, the new media and democratic citizenship. His other books include *Parliament in the Age of the Internet*; *The Electronic Media, Parliament and the People* and *Televised Election Debates; International Perspectives*. He lives in London with his wife, Bernadette, and his cat, Fred.

Key words
To help you find your way around this book, key words are printed in **bold**. You can find some of these words in the glossary on pages 30-31.

Illustrations Alastair Taylor/The Inkshed

This edition 2003

Franklin Watts
96 Leonard Street
London
EC2A 4XD

Franklin Watts Australia
45-51 Huntley Street
Alexandria
NSW 2015

© 2000 Franklin Watts

Designer Magda Weldon
Editor Penny Clarke
Art Director Jonathan Hair
Editor-in-Chief John C. Miles

A CIP catalogue record
for this book is available
from the British Library.

Dewey classification: 351

ISBN 0 7496 5181 4

Printed in Malaysia

Contents

Imagine a society where one person makes all the decisions and everyone else has to carry them out. The one all-powerful person would be a dictator and his or her will would be supreme.

Dictators and fascists

There have been many **dictatorships** in history. Sometimes the **dictator** and the group around him claimed to be appointed by and speaking for God. Or the dictator might be the head of an army that has taken power. In **Fascist** Italy and **Nazi** Germany dictators ruled as if they were supermen. Dictators might allow elections to be held, but only unfair ones in which there is no real opponent to the dictator's rule.

Now let us imagine another kind of society: one where every citizen has a direct say in every major decision.

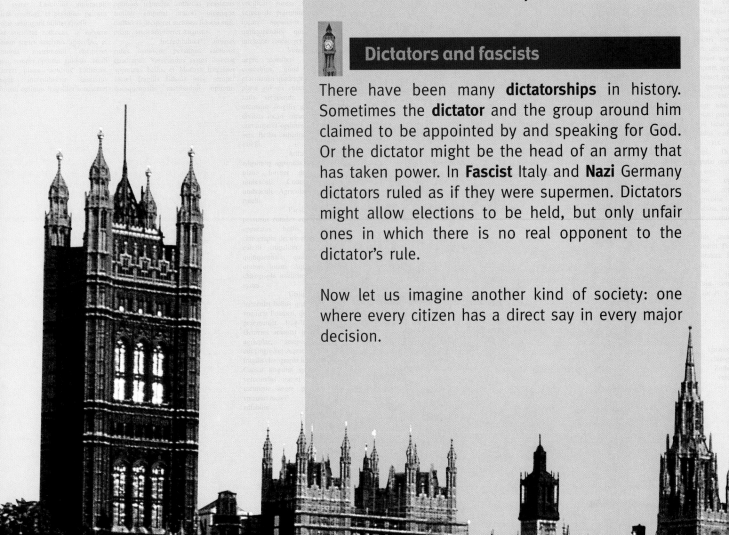

> "Democracy is the worst form of government except all other forms that have been tried."
> **Prime Minister Winston Churchill, 1947**

In Ancient Athens citizens met in the *agora* (marketplace) and made decisions. Most Athenians, such as women and slaves, were not counted as citizens, so 'Athenian **democracy**' was in reality rule by a minority.

 ## Votes for all?

In a vast modern state it would be very difficult for every citizen to think about and vote upon every decision that has to be made. It is easier and more efficient to elect **representatives** to deliberate and vote on our behalf. As long as these representatives are **accountable** to us we can have some control over the decisions being made.

Parliament is the home of **representative democracy**. It is where we citizens send our **chosen representatives** to serve our interests. Unlike a dictatorship, these representatives are appointed by us in fair **elections** and must keep us informed about what they decide and why. We judge their performance at the next election.

Unlike a **direct democracy**, where everyone votes on everything, we give power to our **elected representatives** to act as they see fit in our best interests.

The UK Parliament sits at Westminster, London.

Parliament is made up of three parts. First, there is the **Queen** who is the official **Head of State**. Britain is a **constitutional monarchy** where the Queen only rules symbolically; in reality, power belongs to Parliament. So, although the Queen 'opens' Parliament each year and laws are passed in her name, the Queen herself plays no part in determining decisions made in Parliament.

The second part of Parliament is the **House of Lords**. This used to be the home of the **aristocracy** who inherited the right to sit there, but is now in the process of being reformed.

THE THREE PARTS of Parliament

House of Commons   Head of State   House of Lords

The third part of Parliament is the **House of Commons,** which is elected by the people of the UK. It has 659 Members (called MPs) elected by 659 areas of the country called **constituencies.**

The House of Lords and the House of Commons are situated in the **Houses of Parliament** at **Westminster** in London. The area in London where much Parliamentary business is conducted is known as **Whitehall,** after the street where many government offices are located.

Elections

Elections to the **House of Commons** must take place every five years. Anyone over the age of 18 who is not a convicted criminal, sectioned under mental health legislation or a member of the House of Lords can vote in an election.

Your vote allows you to choose a **representative** from the list of **candidates** 'standing for election' in your **constituency.** Each constituency sends its MP to sit in the House of Commons.

Each time there is a **General Election** (an election of all MPs) there is a new composition of the House of Commons. This is called a new **Parliament** and it sits until the next general election.

Not the only way

There are many ways of running a democracy – the **Parliamentary system** in use in Britain is only one of them – and there is usually room for improvement. But first it is important to understand why democracy matters and how it works. Then, get involved.

Parliament works well when it represents the will of the people.

More than one thousand years ago, Anglo-Saxon kings ruling in Britain summoned the leading aristocrats of the day to the *Witenagemot.* This ancestor of Parliament advised the monarch on laws and taxation.

THIS CARTOON from the late 1800s shows prominent politicians of the day in the lobby of the House of Commons.

A noble assembly

After the Norman Conquest the leading barons and churchmen were called to the King's Council, the *Curia Regis*. The oldest sons of those who regularly attended were summoned to attend after their father's death. This was the origin of the **House of Lords** or **Upper House**, which was based on hereditary power.

Origins of the Commons

The **House of Commons** has its origin in the thirteenth century. In 1265 Simon de Montfort, the chief baron of the day, ordered two knights from each shire (county) to attend the House of Lords and leading figures (burgesses) from the boroughs or 'communes' (commons) to attend a **Lower House**, which became the House of Commons.

In the fourteenth century Parliament came to be consulted on all matters of taxation. In 1376 the **House of Commons** refused to grant the King, Edward III, more money for his war with France and elected one of their Members, Peter de la Mare, to speak on their behalf to the King. He became the first **Speaker of the House** – originally, the member who spoke for the Commons; now the member who presides over the proceedings of the House and ensures that order is kept.

> The only parliament in the world older than the UK's is the Icelandic Athingi.

More power than the Crown?

In the 1600s both King James I and Charles I tried to close down Parliament and rule without it. Eventually, in 1642, **civil war** broke out. The forces of King Charles were defeated by the Parliamentary army led by Oliver Cromwell; Charles was captured and executed. After this it was clear that Parliament was more powerful than whoever wore the crown.

In the 1650s Parliament governed the country without a monarch, but in 1660 the monarchy was restored. In the 1680s there was another conflict before the **Bill of Rights** was made law in 1689. This set out the rights of Parliament and the limits of the monarchy.

Reform, reorganisation

By the early 1800s, the composition of the House of Commons was outdated. Most MPs represented country areas; some represented **boroughs** where there were few voters or one landlord could bribe residents. The new large industrial towns were often not included.

The **Reform Act** of 1832 increased the number of people who could vote and changed the basis upon which people could vote in elections. Later **Reform Acts** gave the vote to most men, but not women. A long struggle by women finally won them the vote in 1928.

The **Parliament Act** of 1911 made it clear that the unelected House of Lords had less power than the elected House of Commons. In the twentieth century the Lords became very much a second chamber and in 1999 most **hereditary peers** lost the right to sit there.

POLITICAL OPPONENTS of the 1640s –
King Charles I and Oliver Cromwell.

MPs are chosen in elections. There are 659 MPs, each representing an area known as a constituency. Each constituency has approximately 60,000 people living in it.

General elections

The election of all MPs is called a **general election**; an election in only one **constituency** (because the elected MP has died or retired) is called a **by-election**. General elections have to take place at least every five years, whenever the Prime Minister of the day asks the Queen to call one.

People are **nominated** as **candidates** to become MPs. Anyone over 21 can be a candidate, if they can find ten people to sign a paper saying they want them to be a candidate and can pay a **deposit** of £500. Although anyone can stand as an **independent candidate**, these are rarely elected. Most people vote for candidates put up by **political parties**.

Running a campaign

It takes lots of energy, time and money to run a successful **election campaign**. This is much easier when candidates are supported by **party organisations**. A **political party** is an organised group of people who share certain **principles** and **policies**. Each party has its own views about how the country should be run. Most people vote for the **candidate** of the party that has views closest to their own.

IN AN ELECTION, the main political parties spend lots of money trying to persuade people to vote for them.

History of the parties

Each party has its own history and policies. The **Conservative (Tory) Party** evolved in the nineteenth century. They support the free market and the right of people to acquire and hold property. The most famous recent Conservative Prime Minister was Margaret Thatcher who was in power between 1979 and 1987.

The **Labour Party** was formed by trade unions to represent their members. It has supported measures to help the least well off.

The Labour government of 1945-51 created the National Health Service and nationalised (brought under public ownership) many industries that were later privatised (sold to private shareholders) by the Thatcher government.

A third party, the **Liberal Democrats**, has a smaller number of MPs. The **Scottish National Party** (SNP) and **Plaid Cymru** support the creation of separate Scottish and Welsh nations.

TRADITIONALLY, the Tory party has been the party of Church, State and landowners; the Labour Party the party of the trade unions.

The three main national parties in the UK are Labour, Conservatives (sometimes called Tories) and the Liberal Democrats.

Parties and elections

During **election campaigns** the parties run national and local campaigns to persuade people to vote for them. In the constituency, they knock on doors, hold meetings, go around the streets with loudspeaker vans and write to or phone everyone.

On **election day** the people cast their votes for the candidate of their choice and the one who receives the highest number of votes becomes the MP.

An MP (Member of Parliament) is a representative of his or her community. The MP's constituents have a right to expect their representative to look after their interests.

Speaking to your MP

MPs run regular **surgeries**. Like doctor's surgeries, where patients bring their medical problems to their GP, the MP's **constituency surgery** offers a chance for anyone to make an appointment and speak to their MP about an issue.

Party members

As well as being constituency representatives, MPs are **party members**. They are expected to vote with their **party**. Each week the party managers – called the **Whips** – send MPs a list of what Parliamentary business and debates are coming up in the next week.

Some items on the list are underlined once (a **one-line whip**) – it is not urgent for MPs to be in the Commons chamber to vote. Other items are underlined twice (a **two-line whip**) – MPs' attendance is expected. A **three-line whip** means that MPs must attend and vote with their party.

When there is a **three-line whip** MPs arrive from all over the country – sometimes MPs who have been in hospital have been transported in by ambulance!

MPs have offices in Parliament and this is where they do their own work, talking to constituents, preparing speeches and meeting people.

Before the 1997 elections there were more MPs called John than there were women. Since 1997 there have been 121 women MPs sitting in Parliament.

MPs HOLD regular surgeries, such as this one, where constituents can discuss issues that concern them.

The chamber of the House of Commons is where they go to **debate** issues and vote. MPs also spend a lot of time in **committees** where they examine laws in detail and inspect the work of the various **government departments**.

A busy life

Most MPs lead very busy lives. They spend some time in their constituencies and the rest in Parliament. They must make regular speeches as well as media appearances. They need to have their own views, but must be prepared to listen to their constituents and support their party. There is no training for MPs – no apprenticeship you can take up to learn the skills of being a good MP.

Where do they come from?

MPs come from all walks of life: teachers, lawyers, doctors, computer experts, journalists, trade unionists, business people. But it is still not the case that the composition of Parliament reflects society.

MPs have to be at Westminster sometimes and in their constituencies at other times. Time at Westminster is split between their offices, the House of Commons and committee work.

AN MP'S DAY can be a blur of train travel, sitting in committee meetings and giving television interviews.

Monday

**7.00 am
Catch train from constituency to London. Read the local and national newspapers on the way.**

**9.00
Arrive at office in Westminster. Look at the post.
Attend select committee meeting.**

"The British public . . .
have taken it for
granted that MPs are
self–serving
impostors and
hypocrites who put
party before country
and self before
party."
Ivor Crewe
addressing the
Nolan Inquiry
into Standards
in Public Life,
17 January, 1995

1.00 pm
Lunch with directors of a company thinking of locating a new plant in the constituency.
Attend chamber for debate.
Called out of debate to be interviewed by TV station about an environmental problem that might affect the constituency. Division bell rings to signal a vote. Rush from TV interview.

4.00
Meet Minister from Department of Environment in Division Lobby, where MPs vote. Ask for a meeting to discuss constituency problem.

4.10
Attend meeting in Whips' office. Return to office to deal with correspondence and work on speech for debate on Wednesday.

6.00
Attend All–Party Internet group meeting. Dinner with MPs from two neighbouring constituencies in Members' dining room. Discuss common approach to environmental problem. Newspaper wants a comment for tomorrow morning's edition – fax press release from office.

9.20
Return to London flat – phone family, watch news and read papers for tomorrow.

Parliament represents the people. Government runs the country. Being an MP is not the same thing as being in the Government. The party that has more seats than all the others runs the country.

1992

Conservative Party	Labour Party	Liberal Democrats	Other parties
336 seats	271 seats	24 seats	20 seats

1997

Conservative Party	Labour Party	Liberal Democrats	Other parties
165 seats	419 seats	46 seats	29 seats

2001

Conservative Party	Labour Party	Liberal Democrats	Other parties
166 seats	413 seats	52 seats	28 seats

HOW PARLIAMENT can change – the results of the 1992, 1997 and 2001 elections.

For example, after the 1992 election the largest party, the Conservatives, had 21 more seats than all the others. This is called a **majority**. With such a majority they could out-vote all the other parties, so they formed the **Government**. Their party leader, John Major, became the Prime Minister.

After the 1997 general election the picture was rather different: the Labour Party had a majority of 179 and its leader, Tony Blair, became Prime Minister. All parties aim to win a majority of seats. When they do, they become the Government.

Parliament opens

Each November the Queen, as **Head of State**, opens Parliament. She reads a speech, called the **Queen's Speech**, setting out the policies that her **Government** will be making laws about.

The Government proposes most of the laws that are debated in Parliament. Leading members of the Government, called **Ministers**, specialise in different areas of **policy**.

When laws are proposed, Ministers argue the case for them. They sit on the front benches of the Government side in the House of Commons, so they are called **frontbenchers**. MPs who are not Ministers are known as **backbenchers**.

EVERY NOVEMBER, in full ceremonial dress, the Queen opens Parliament.

"People need
to feel a sense of
belonging
. . . the role of State and
Government will alter;
the citizen is a citizen
because he or she is
part of
a society."
Tony Blair,
New Year,
2000

Opposition

On the other side of the Commons chamber are the **Opposition party** MPs. Their job is to oppose the Government. The biggest Opposition party sits directly across from the Government benches and its frontbenchers are known as **Shadow Ministers**, who argue against Government proposals.

Government departments

Most of Government's work is carried on outside Parliament in various **Government Departments**. These are sometimes known as **Whitehall**, after the street in which many of them are based.

Votes of confidence

As long as Governments have a majority in Parliament they stay in power. If they lose a vote there usually follows a **Vote of Confidence**. If that is lost the Prime Minister calls an election so that the public can elect a new Government.

Laws are rules that everyone in the country must obey. In a democracy nobody is above the law. About one hundred new laws are passed each year. How does Parliament make new laws?

Laws in the making

The vast majority of proposals for new laws come from the Government. A proposed new law is called a **Bill**. Before the Government puts its Bill to Parliament much work will have been done. It is likely to have consulted with the public via a **Green Paper** or outlined its policy in a **White Paper**. Ministers in the Department in charge of the Bill will have met with interested people. Government lawyers will have spent a good deal of time making sure that the Bill says exactly what the Government intends it to say.

Readings and standing committees

The Bill is introduced by a **First Reading**. This is simply an official notice that a Bill is going to be proposed and what it's about. It gives MPs time to prepare to discuss it.

THE STAGES of a Bill's progress through Parliament

First reading

Second reading

House of Lords

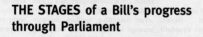

Standing committees

Third reading

Royal Assent

THE RESULT of a vote is announced to the House of Commons. The Speaker of the House sits at the end between the two rows of Government and Opposition benches.

Stages in a Bill's passage through Parliament are called Readings because originally all proposed laws had to be read out. Printing had not been invented and most MPs were illiterate.

Shortly afterwards comes the **Second Reading**. At this point the principles of the Bill are considered on the floor of the House. The Bill is then usually sent to be looked at in detail by a **Standing Committee**.

Standing committees are small groups of MPs (about eleven on each one) who are appointed to examine Bills in detail. The composition of standing committees reflects that of the whole House – so the Government has a majority and can defend its Bill. It is at this stage that amendments can be proposed to the Bill.

If a Bill is really controversial, the House of Commons turns itself into a **Committee of the Whole House** – one big Standing Committee made up of all MPs. This rarely happens.

The final stages

At the **Third Reading** the Bill is debated and there is a vote – known as a division. MPs file through the **Division Lobbies,** one for the 'Ayes' (for those supporting the Bill) and the other for the 'Noes' (for those in opposition). The numbers passing through each division lobby are counted. If the Government has a **majority**, the Bill is then passed to the **House of Lords** for its consideration. If the Lords vote against the Bill it is returned to the Commons for **amendment**.

Once a **Bill** has passed through both Houses, it is sent to the Queen for the **Royal Assent**. By convention, the Queen agrees to any law passed by Parliament. Once it has Royal Assent the Bill becomes an **Act of Parliament**. It is the law of the land.

The most important person in Parliament is the Prime Minister. He or she has three jobs: head of the Government, leader of his or her party and MP, representing a constituency like any other MP.

The chief Minister

Unlike a President, the **Prime Minister** is not **Head of State**. Technically, he or she is the Queen's chief Minister and head of the Government. At one time, monarchs did not have Prime Ministers.

Tony Blair is the youngest Prime Minister since William Pitt the Younger in the 1700s. The oldest was William Gladstone who was 83 when he took office for the fourth time in 1892.

THE CABINET meets every Thursday morning in the Cabinet Room at 10 Downing Street, the Prime Minister's official London residence.

George I, who came from Germany, became King in 1714 and spoke little English. He had little interest in British politics and spent half of each year away from the country. So, he came to depend upon the leading politicians in his Government, the leader of whom became the **Prime Minister**.

Robert Walpole, who was the King's chief Minister from 1721 to 1742, is usually regarded as the first British Prime Minister.

The Cabinet

Prime Ministers have the power to appoint and dismiss **Ministers**. In short, they decide who will serve in the key positions of Government.

The most important Ministers, with responsibilities for key areas of national life, are appointed to the Prime Minister's **Cabinet**. This is the main government **committee** which meets every Thursday morning.

The job of the **Cabinet** is to determine **policy** to be put to Parliament and to oversee the Government Departments and the overall work of managing the country.

This task is too big for one committee meeting once a week, so the Cabinet has many **sub-committees** looking at particular aspects of government policy.

Policy and PMs

The **Prime Minister**'s power arises from the fact that, as head of the Government, he is in overall charge of determining **policy,** and as leader of the **majority party** he can ensure that his policies win the day in Parliament.

One of Parliament's two main tasks is to make the law. The other is to hold Government to account – to find out what the Government is doing and to question Ministers on their work.

Questions for the house

All **Ministers** must attend Parliament regularly and answer **questions** about the work of their Departments. MPs can ask questions of Ministers, either verbally on the floor of the House or in writing. These questions are intended to ensure that everything that the Government does is **open to criticism** from the representatives of the people.

Opposition MPs will usually seek to show how much better they could run the country than the Minister being questioned. MPs from particular areas will ask questions on behalf of their **regions** or **local constituents**. This is one of the most effective and public opportunities that MPs have to question leading members of the Government.

Question Time

The most publicised question period occurs every Wednesday afternoon when the **Prime Minister** answers questions on the floor of the House. It is usually a noisy and excitable event, covered live on TV and radio, in which the key policies of the Government are debated before the nation.

The **Leader of the Opposition** is able to put several questions to the Prime Minister during this period and it is often regarded as a high-profile contest between the main parties.

QUESTION TIME takes place on Wednesday afternoons. Here, Prime Minister Tony Blair stands to give an answer.

Other types of scrutiny

More effective opportunities for Parliamentary scrutiny occur in the **select committees**. These exist to examine specific aspects of Government policy. Select committees are made up of MPs from all parties and enquire into any subject they wish. In the course of their inquiries select committees can call witnesses and ask to see documents.

The purpose of select committee inquiries is to see how well the Government is doing and offer proposals for better **policies**. Select committees publish reports on each inquiry.

Individual MPs can write to Ministers on behalf of their constituents and often raise **constituents' questions** and concerns with Ministers when they are being questioned in the House.

The UK Parliament sits for more days and for longer hours than any other parliament in the world.

Any member of the public can visit Parliament and see it in action. You can write to your MP and ask for a ticket to the 'Stranger's Gallery', which is where the public sits.

Since 1996 Parliament has been online – at www. parliament.uk – and www.explore. parliament.uk for young people

Parliament and the press

Sitting above the Commons chamber, in the **Press Gallery**, are a number of journalists called the **Press Lobby**. It is their job to report the affairs of Parliament to the world outside. Most people receive information about Parliament from the newspapers, radio and television.

Reporting Parliament was not always allowed. MPs once held the view that what they discussed in Parliament was no business of the people. In 1811 a printer called Thomas **Hansard** started to publish daily reports of what went on in Parliament.

Into the modern world

In 1884 reporters were allowed into the Parliamentary press gallery. Newspapers published long, daily accounts of the previous day's proceedings.

By 1978 radio microphones were allowed in so that, for the first time, people at home could hear the sound of their MPs in debate. In 1985 the House of Lords allowed cameras and in 1989 the House of Commons also entered the TV age. It is now possible to see proceedings without ever having to visit Westminster. The TV channel **BBC Parliament** shows nothing but Parliament at work.

HANSARD'S
PARLIAMENTARY DEBATES:

THIRD SERIES,

COMMENCING WITH THE ACCESSION OF

WILLIAM IV.

10° & 11° VICTORIÆ, 1847.

VOL. XCIV.

COMPRISING THE PERIOD FROM

THE SEVENTH TO THE TWENTY-THIRD
DAY OF JULY, 1847.

Sixth and last Volume of the Session.

LONDON:
PRINTED AND PUBLISHED FOR MR. HANSARD,
BY G. WOODFALL AND SON, ANGEL COURT, SKINNER STREET;
AND BY
LONGMAN AND CO.; C. DOLMAN; J. RODWELL; J. BOOTH; HATCHARD AND SON;
J. RIDGWAY; CALKIN AND BUDD; J. BIGG AND SON; J. BAIN; J. M. RICHARD-
SON; P. RICHARDSON; ALLEN AND CO.; AND R. BALDWIN.

1847.

HANSARD is the official record of Parliamentary transactions. Here is an example from 1847.

Many MPs complain that the public sees too little of them. Big **debates** and dramatic moments from **Prime Minister's Question Time** often make the main news broadcasts, but much of the work of MPs takes place in the less heated debates and in committees which are not often shown on TV.

New technology

With the rise of new technologies such as the **Internet**, it is much easier for citizens to find out about the affairs of Parliament. **Hansard** has been on the web since 1996.

It is now possible to write to MPs by **e-mail** and look at web sites run by the media, parties, pressure groups and individual MPs. It is possible to have your say in **electronic discussions**, which allow groups of citizens to feed their expertise into the democratic process.

The public image

Politicians and parties are eager to ensure that their public image is a positive one, so they appoint **media managers**, known as **'spin doctors'**, to make sure that reporters see things from their point of view. Journalists don't believe everything that **spin doctors** tell them, but at least they know what bias to expect. Most political journalism is partly a matter of interpretation: not everyone will see the same event the same way.

How does all of this compare with the rest of the world? Democracy takes different forms in different countries – although in some parts of the world democratic parliaments have yet to come about.

The USA

The United States is a **federal** state. Each of the fifty states within the Union makes its own state laws, but laws affecting all of them (**federal laws**) are made in the **Congress**, made up of two elected assemblies: the **House of Representatives**, which has 435 members elected every two years, and the **Senate**, which has 100 members, two for each state. There is also a federal **President**, elected every four years, who is the **Head of State** and **Chief Executive** – a very different arrangement from the UK.

Germany

THE BUNDESTAG, or German Parliament, meets at its new headquarters in Berlin.

Also a **federal** state, Germany has different regions, called **lande.** Each has its own elected assembly. The lande send members to the Upper House of the German Parliament, the **Bundesrat.** The nationally elected **Bundestag** has 669 members. It is one of the only parliaments in the world with more members than the British House of Commons (which has 659 members).

In 1706 the Scottish Parliament was closed down and Scottish MPs went to sit at Westminster. 293 years later a new Scottish Parliament came into being.

The European Union

Since 1973 the UK has been a member of the **European Economic Union** (since called the **European Union** or **EU**). This is a group of European nations that have joined together to create one big market for their goods and services and have agreed to accept **common laws** in relation to some matters. The EU is not a **federal state** – the fifteen member states of the EU are independent nations.

There is a **European Parliament** based in Strasbourg which has 626 members, elected across Europe every four years. Its role is to oversee the work of the **European Commission**, which initiates EU policy, and to ensure that the interests of European citizens are taken into account.

Having a parliament for Europe as well as the UK is a new development. Some support it because it helps to bring Europeans closer together. Others worry that the EU will become stronger than the national parliaments and governments.

Devolution in the UK

Also new are the **devolved parliaments and assemblies** within the UK, set up in the late 1990s. Scotland now has its own Parliament, with 129 members elected to make laws on most matters concerning life in Scotland. Some powers, such as defence and foreign policy, still remain with the UK Parliament. Wales and Northern Ireland also have devolved assemblies.

The principle of **devolution** is that government should take place as close to people as possible. So, each nation within the UK makes decisions about matters that affect only them, the UK makes laws about matters that affect the entire population and the EU makes laws on some matters concerning all Europeans.

Act A law passed by Parliament.

Bill A draft Act of Parliament.

Cabinet The Prime Minister's committee, composed of leading Ministers within the Government.

Chamber The hall in which the House of Commons sits – the House of Lords sits in a separate chamber.

committees Groups of MPs who meet to consider something. In Parliament there are standing committees, which consider Bills and select committees, which examine the work of specific Government Departments.

constituency An electoral area which elects an MP. There are 659 in the UK with approximately 60,000 people in each.

democracy A system of rule in which the views of the people are of greatest importance.

dictatorship Power held by one person or party without elections or accountability.

election An opportunity for citizens to vote for parties, policies and candidates.

European Union A community of European nations (currently 15) within a single market and legal framework.

Government The central policy-making body (the executive) made up of the Prime Minister, the Cabinet, Ministers and their Departments.

Hansard The daily Official Report of what has been said in Parliament, available in paper form and on the Internet.

legislation Making the law.

majority One more than half voting; so, if 420 MPs vote on a subject and 150 vote against with 270 voting for, the majority in favour is 120 – the difference between 150 and 270.

Minister A member of the Government with responsibility for an area of policy.

MP An elected member of the House of Commons.

Opposition The biggest party that is not the Government. Currently the Conservatives, they are known formally as 'Her Majesty's Loyal Opposition'.

party An organised group of people who agree on a set of principles and policies.

Press Lobby Journalists who are given permission to report within Parliament.

Prime Minister The leader of the Government and the main party in the House of Commons. The official title is 'First Lord of the Treasury'.

Queen's Speech Annual talk to Parliament by the Head of State in which she outlines the Government's programme of law-making for the year ahead.

representative A person elected by other people to act on their behalf.

spin doctors Party media managers.

Whips Party business managers who must make sure that MPs on their side speak and vote in the interest of the party.

PICTURE CREDITS
Cover image: Popperfoto/Reuters (Kieran Doherty)
Mary Evans Picture Library p. 10
Terry Moore pp. 15, 21
Parliamentary Education Unit pp. 6-7, 25 (Graeme Quin)
Popperfoto/Reuters pp. 1, 3, 5, 19 (Kieran Doherty), 22 (Fiona Hanson), 28
Rex Features p. 12 (Andrew Price)